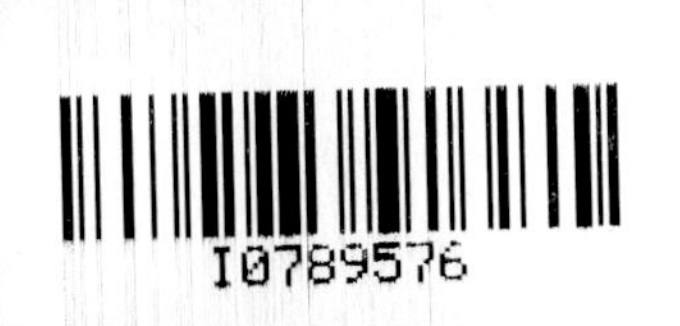

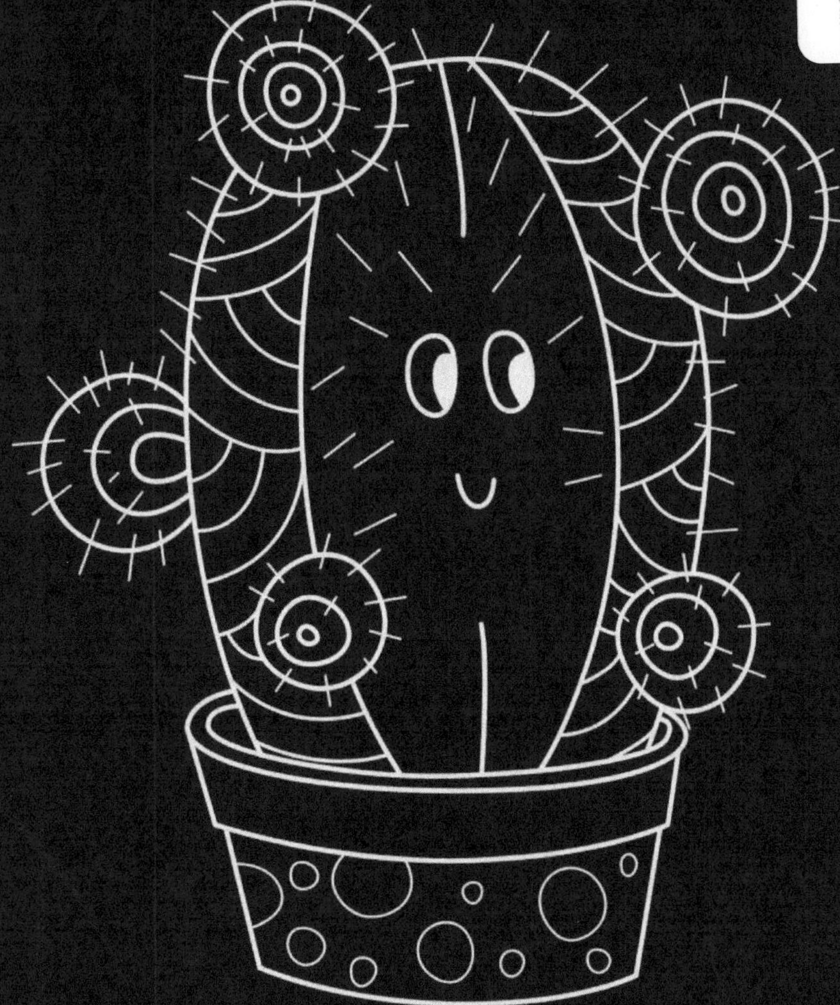

TINY CACTUS PUBLISHING

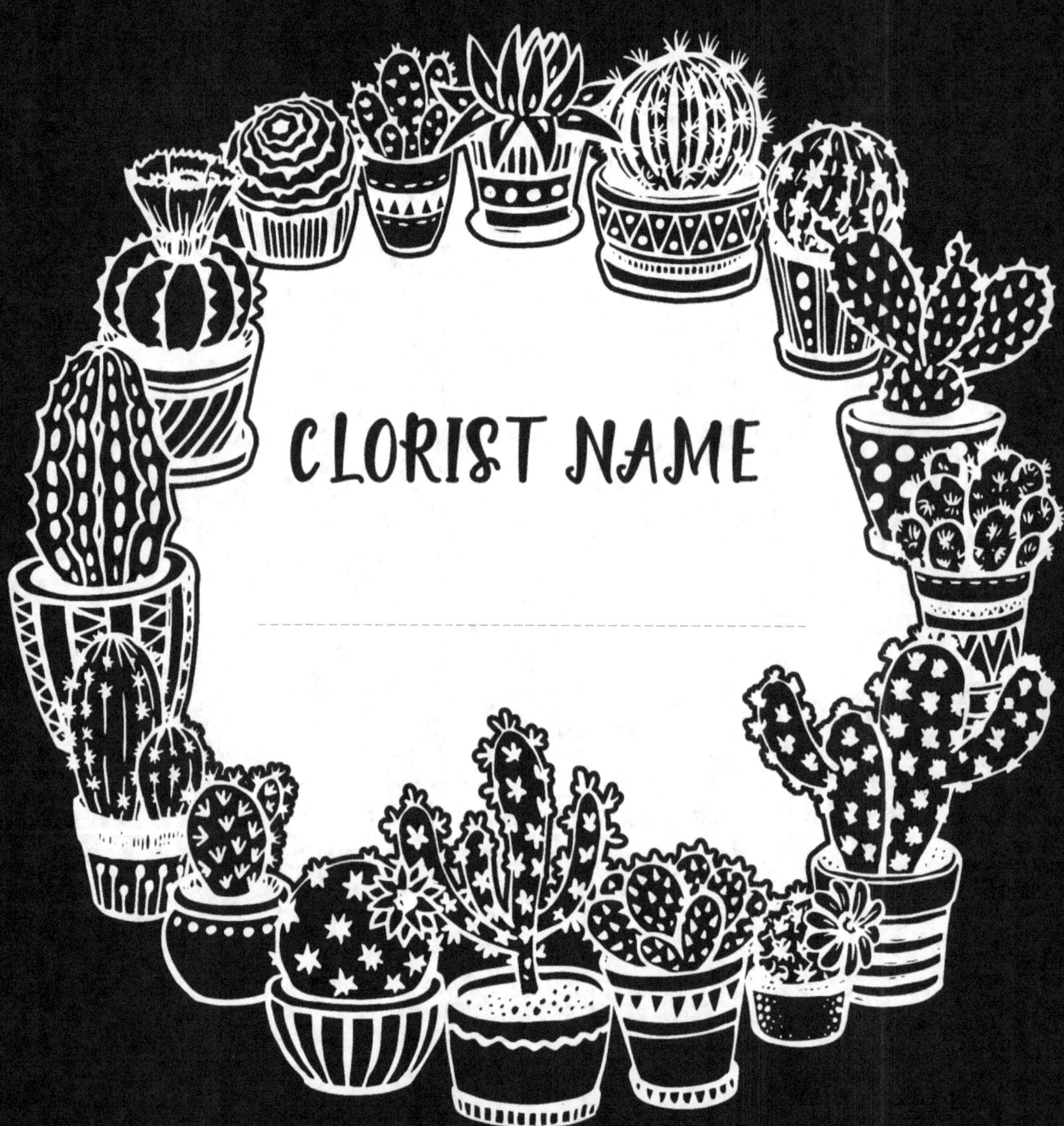
CLORIST NAME

TEST PAGE

PREPARE YOUR COLOR

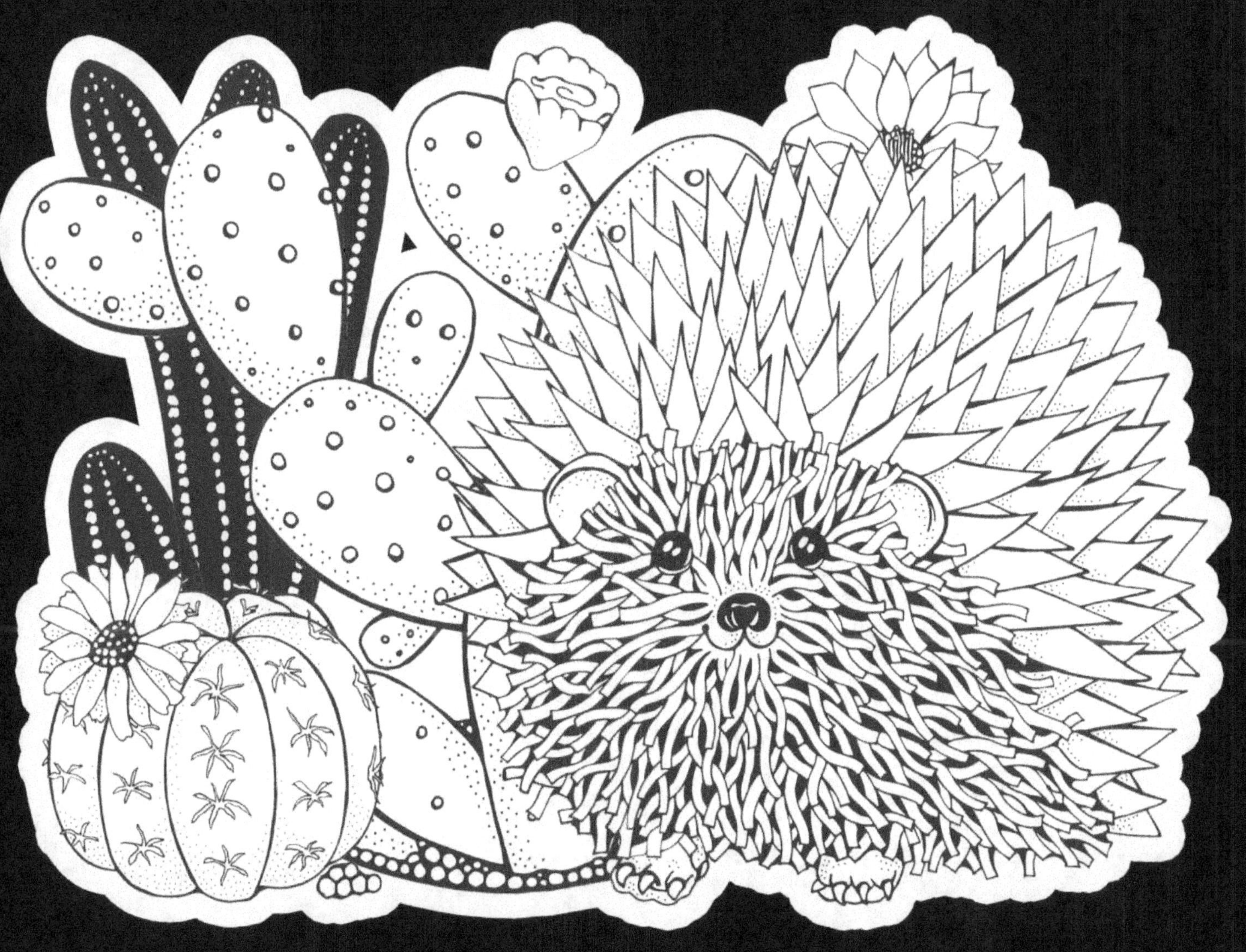

WARM UP !!

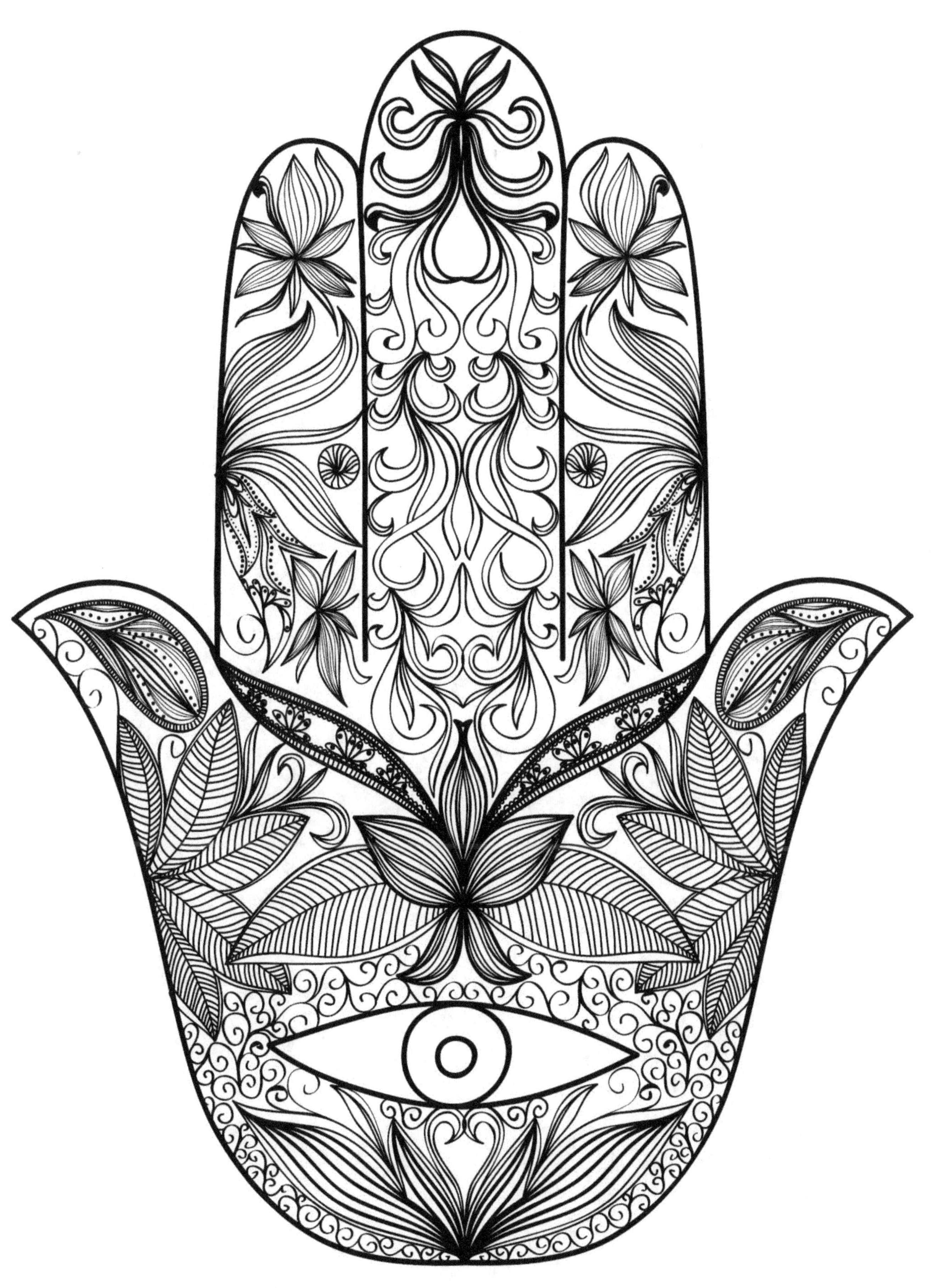

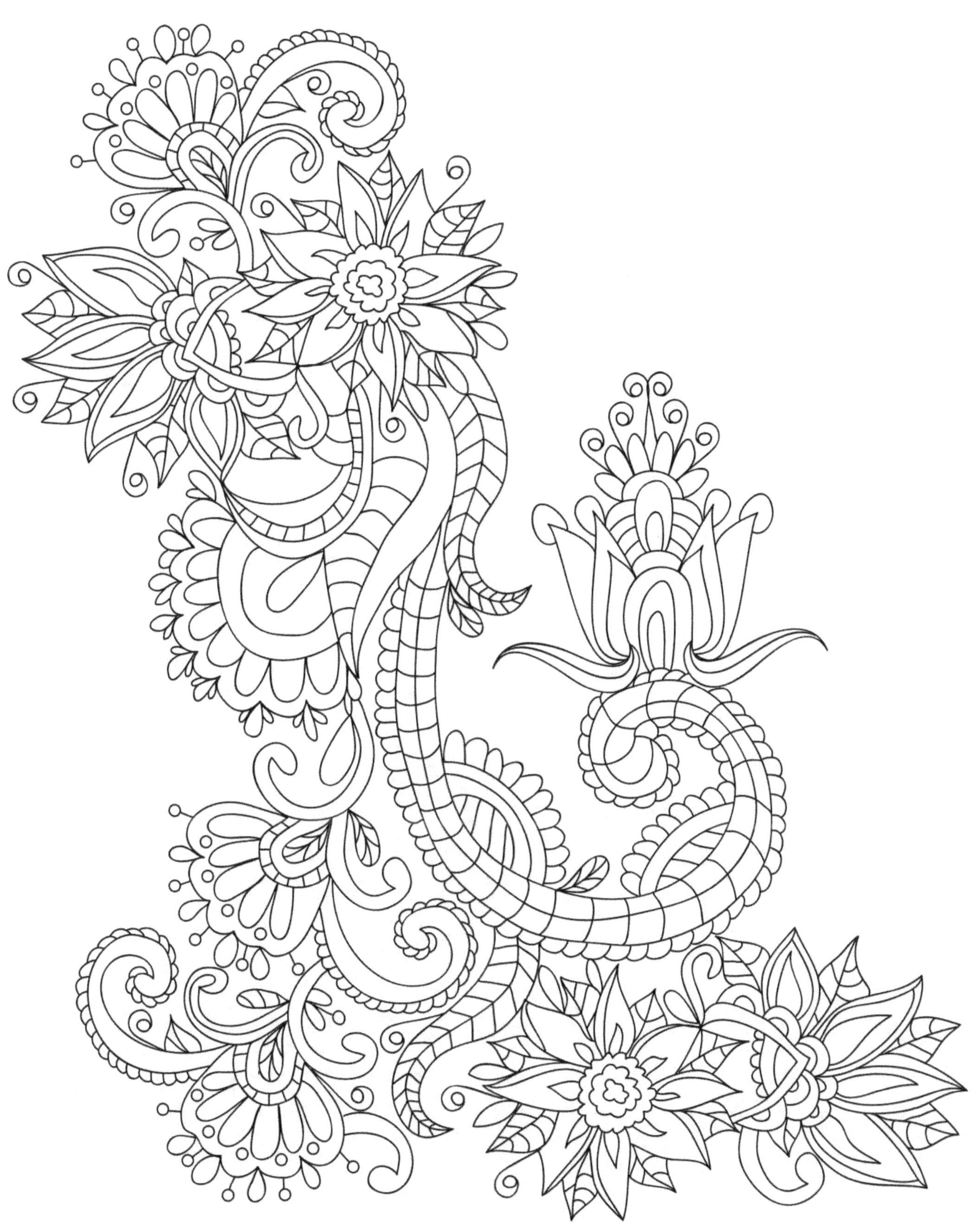

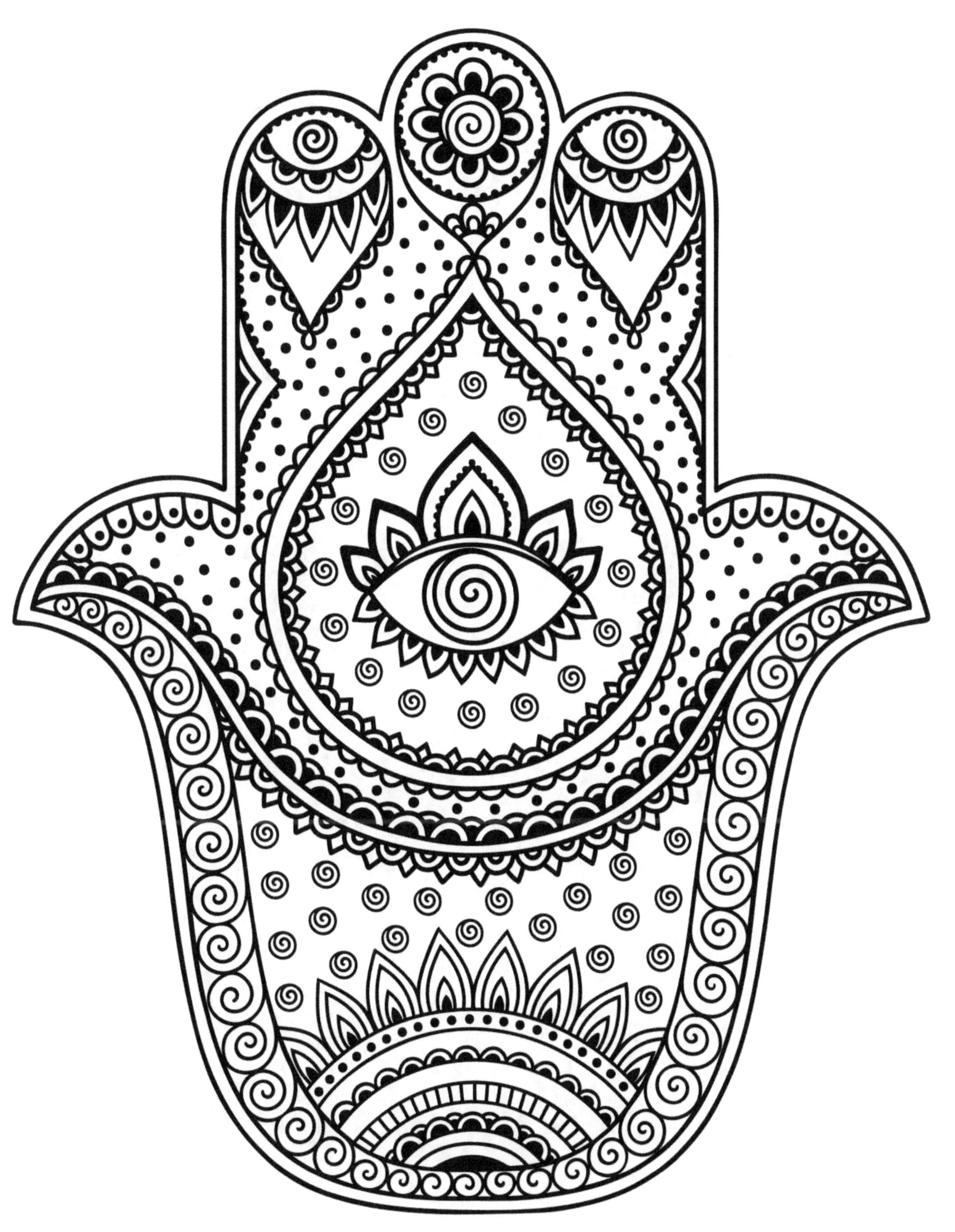

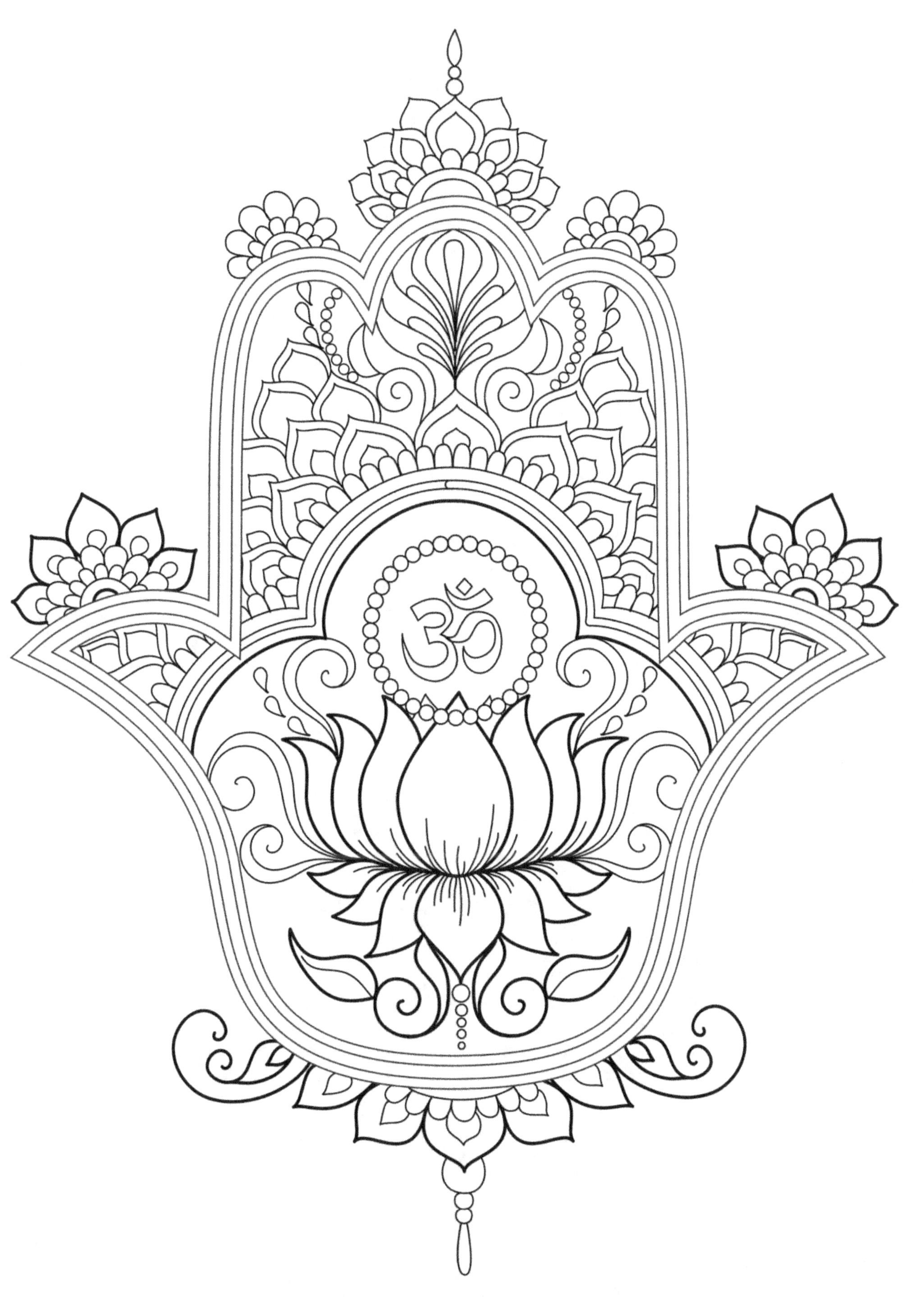

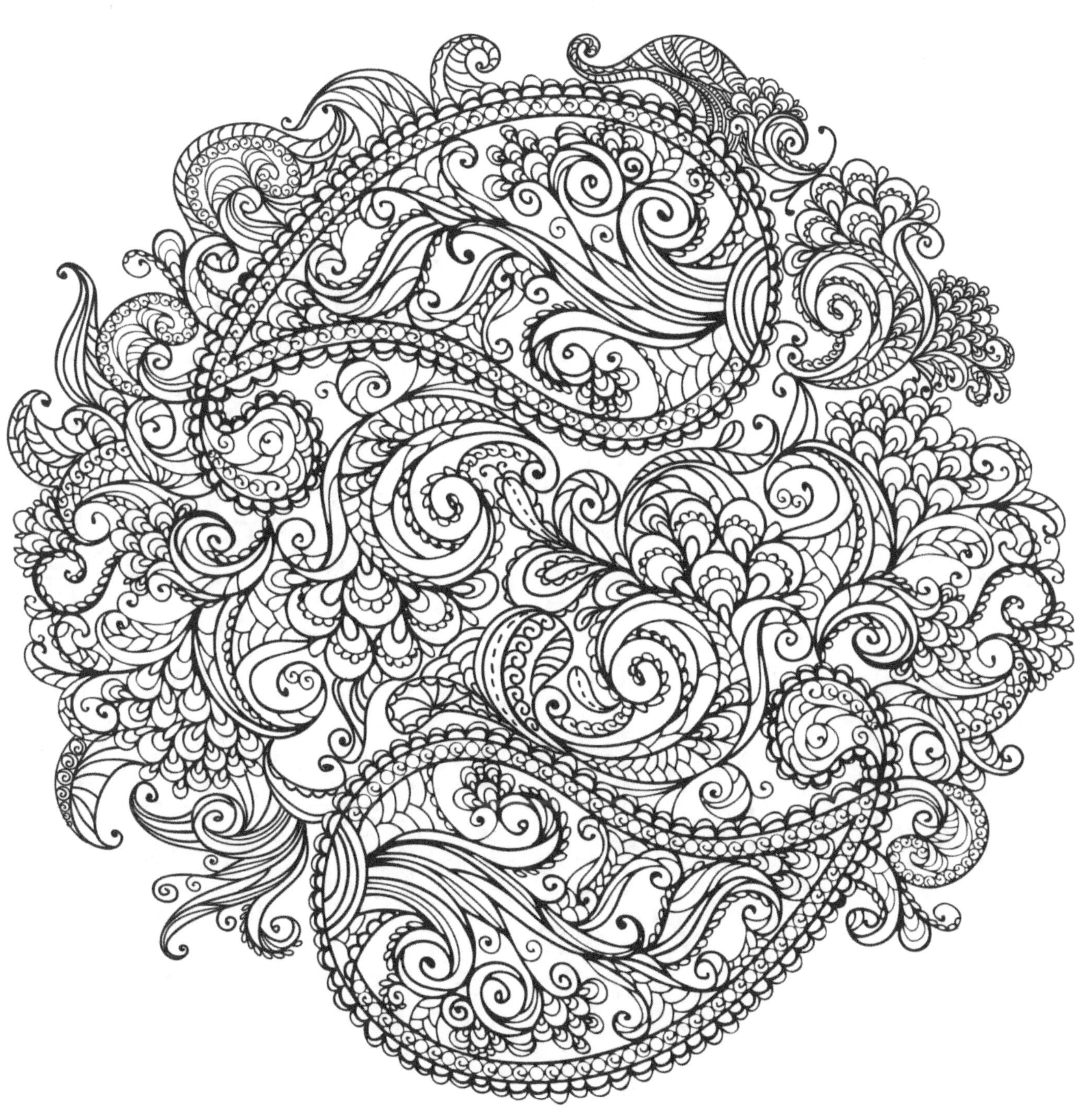

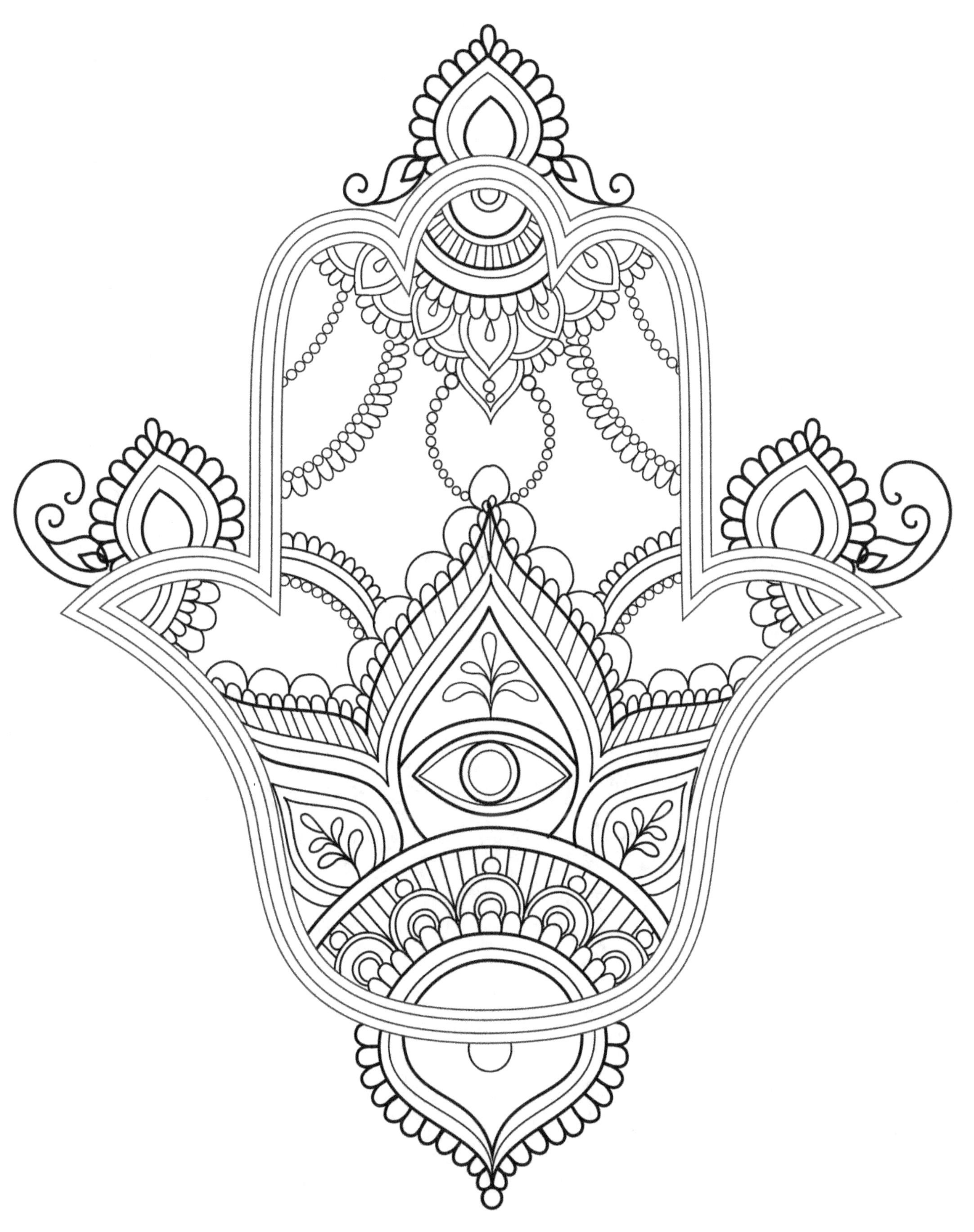

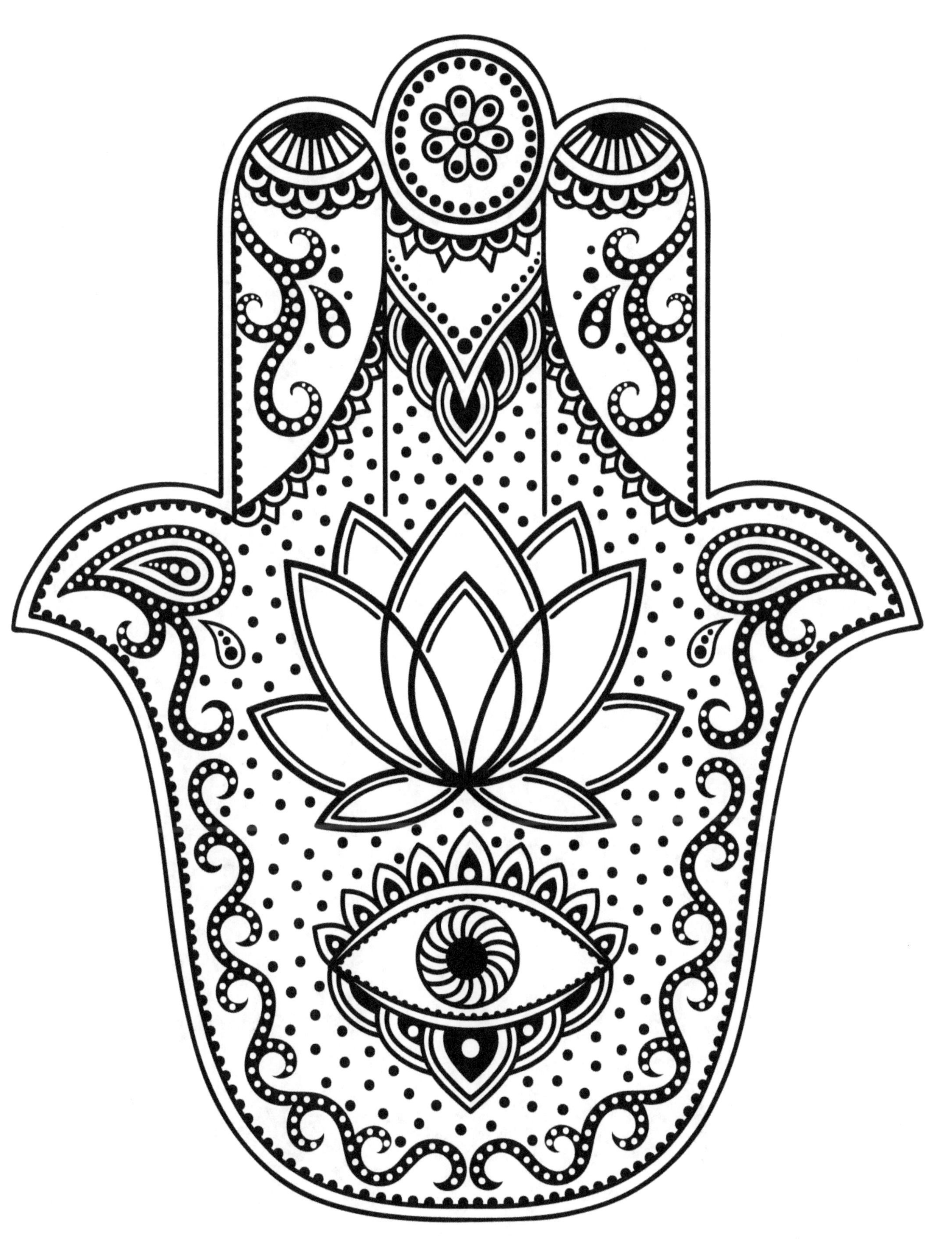

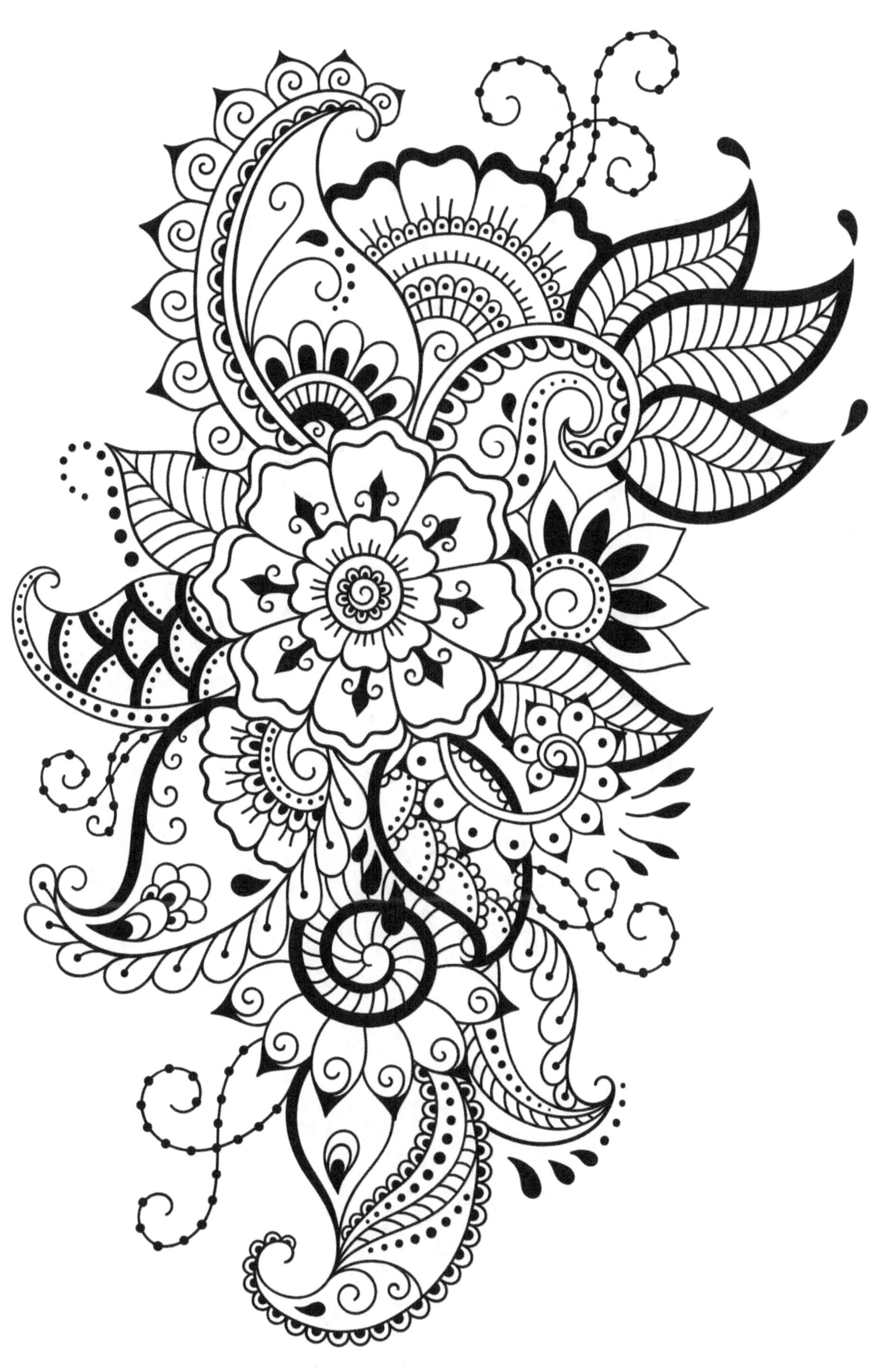

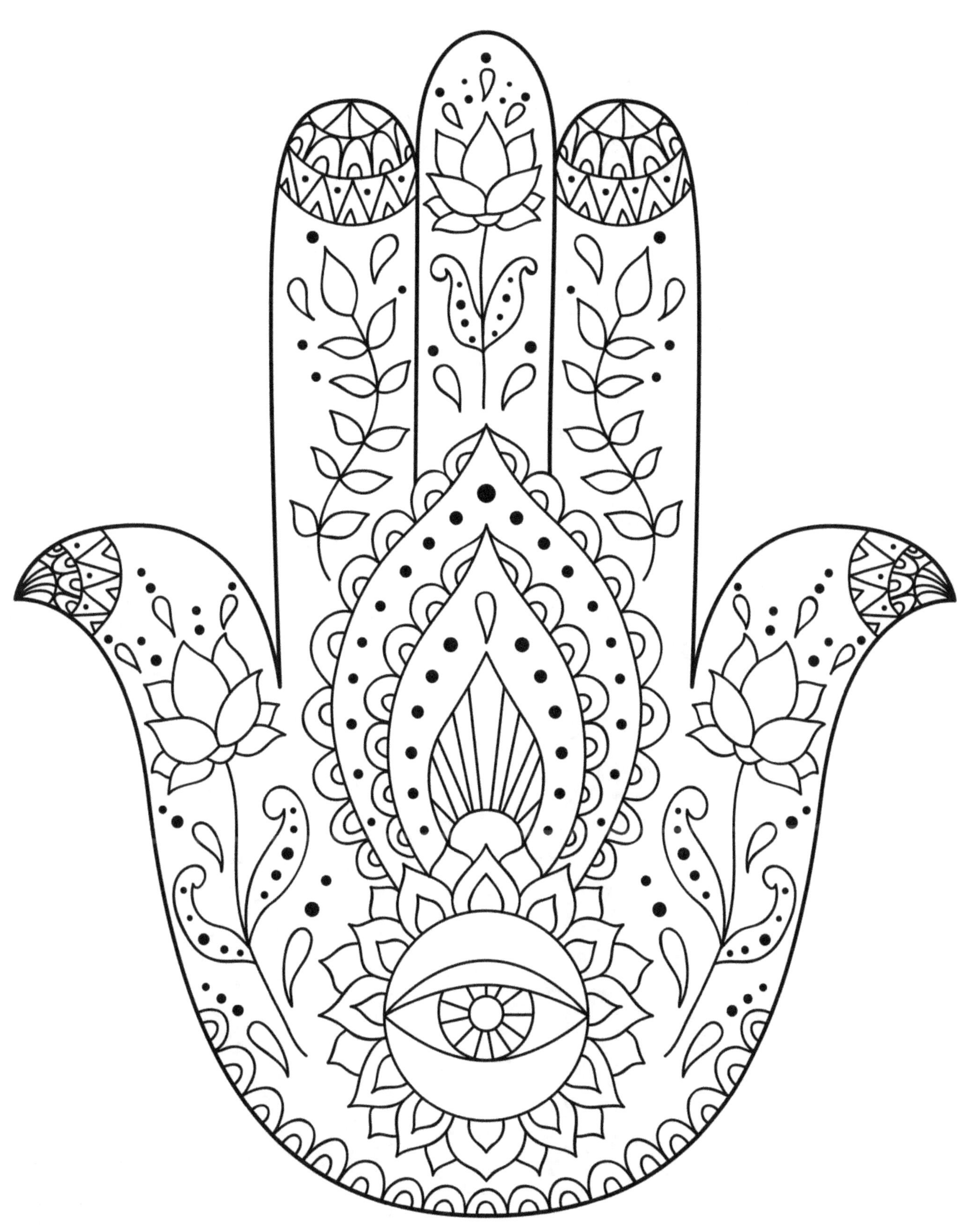

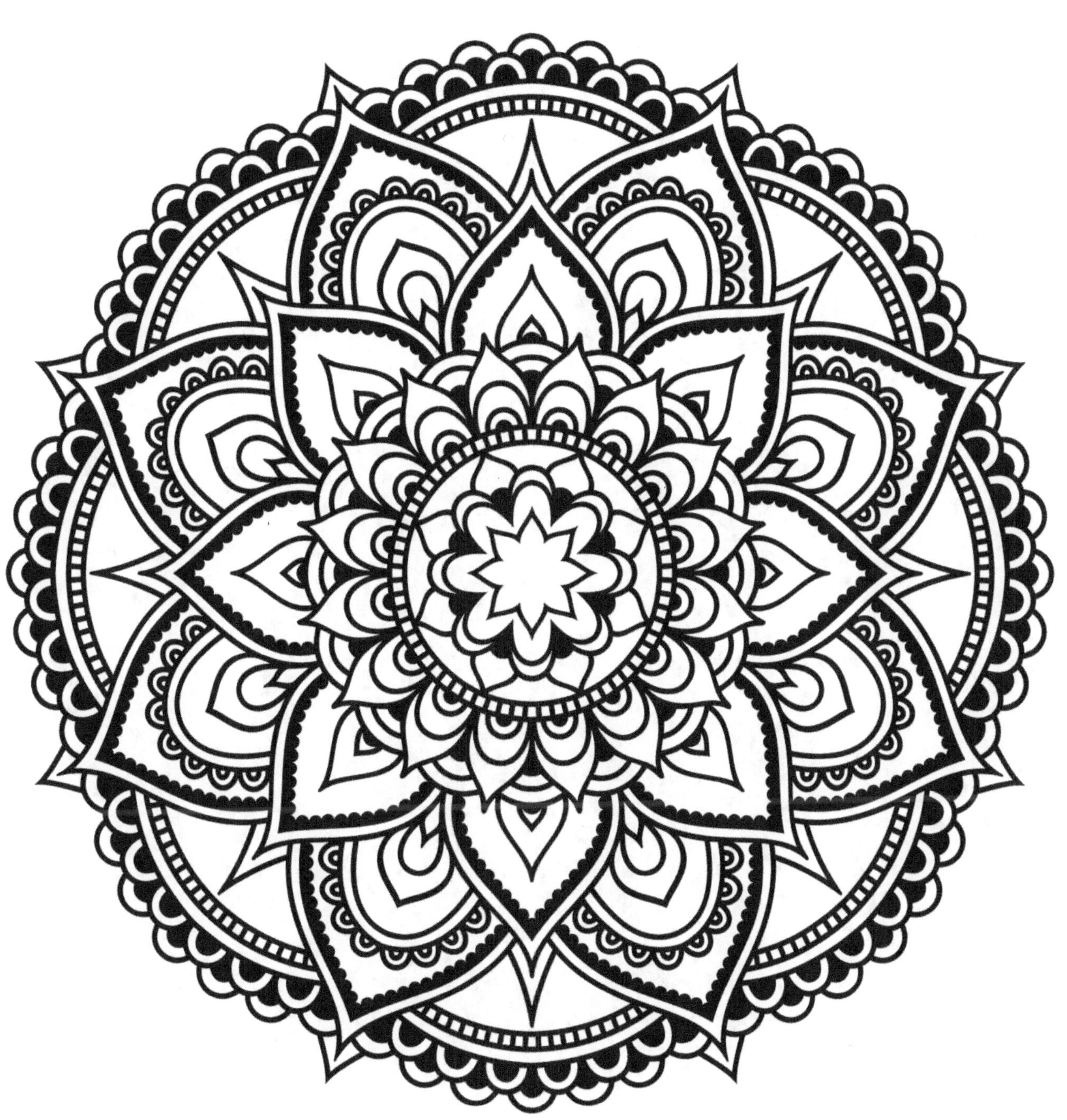

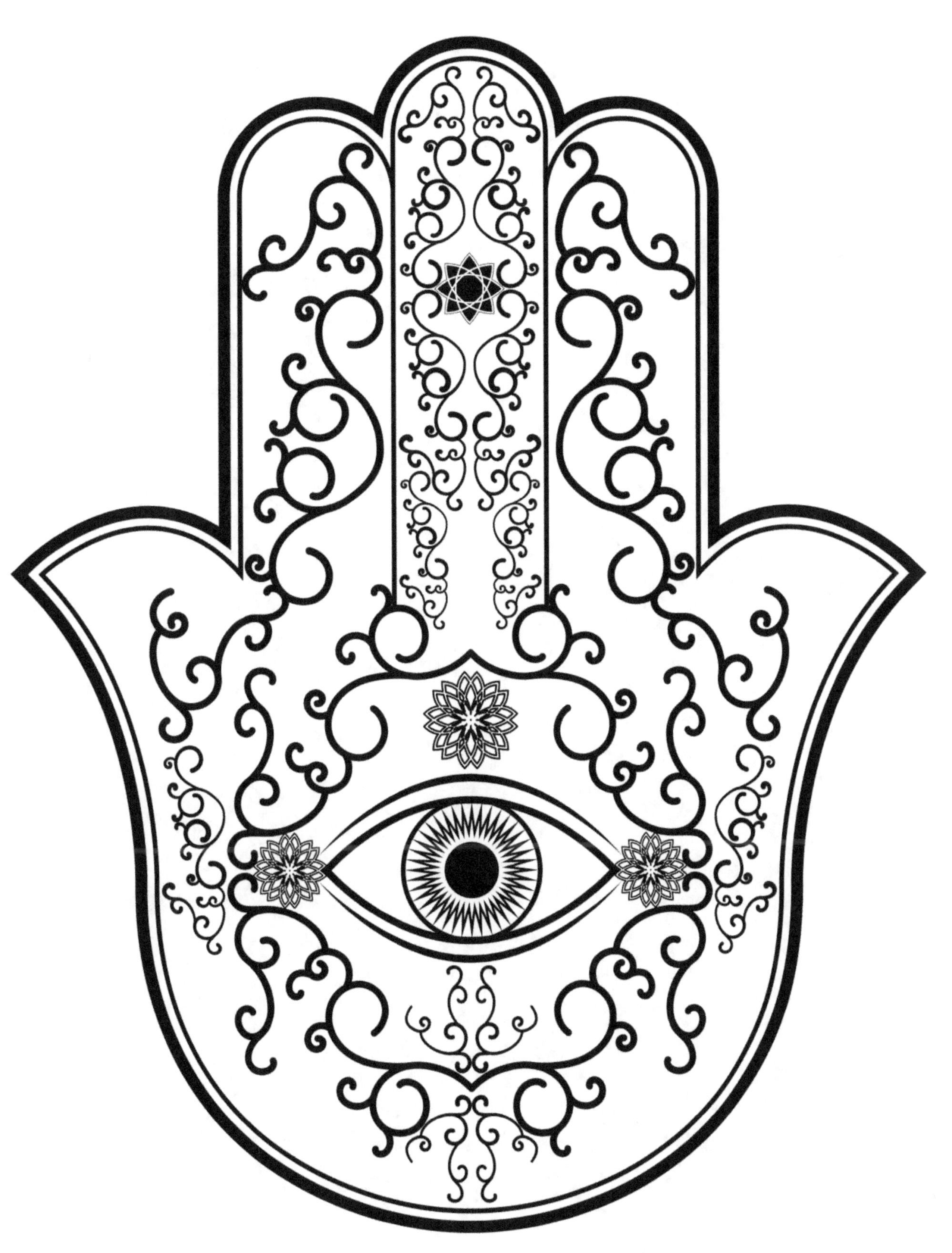

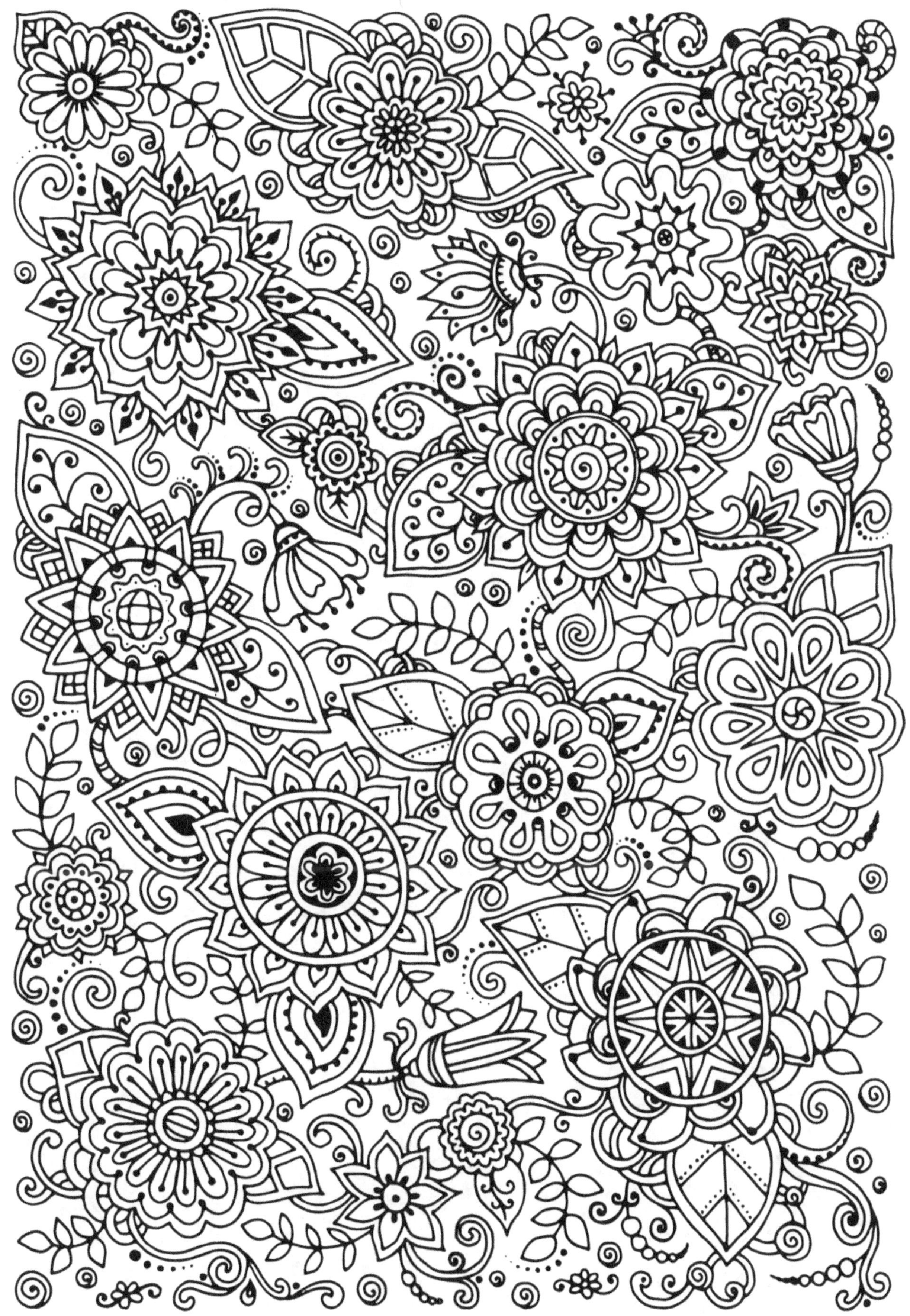

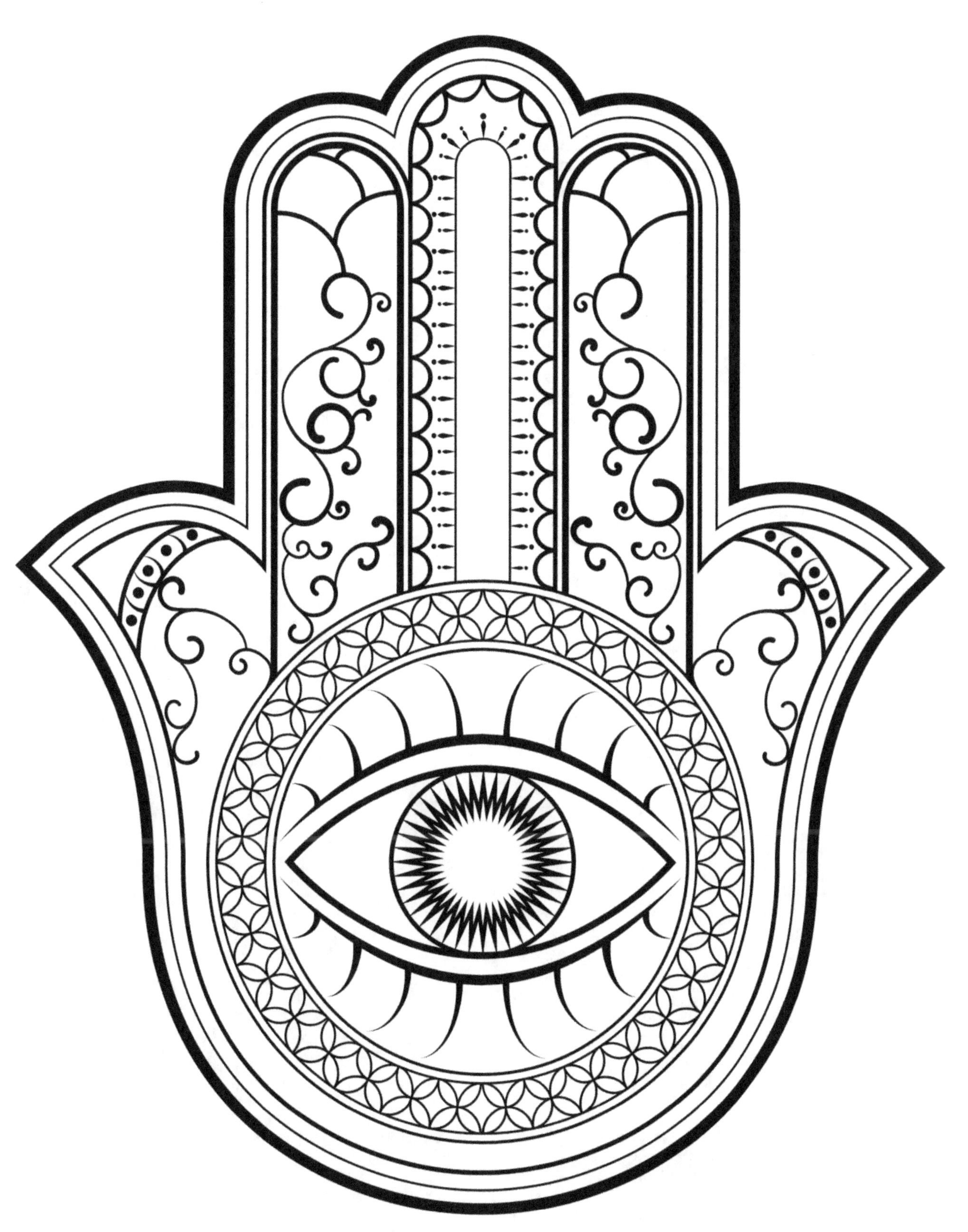

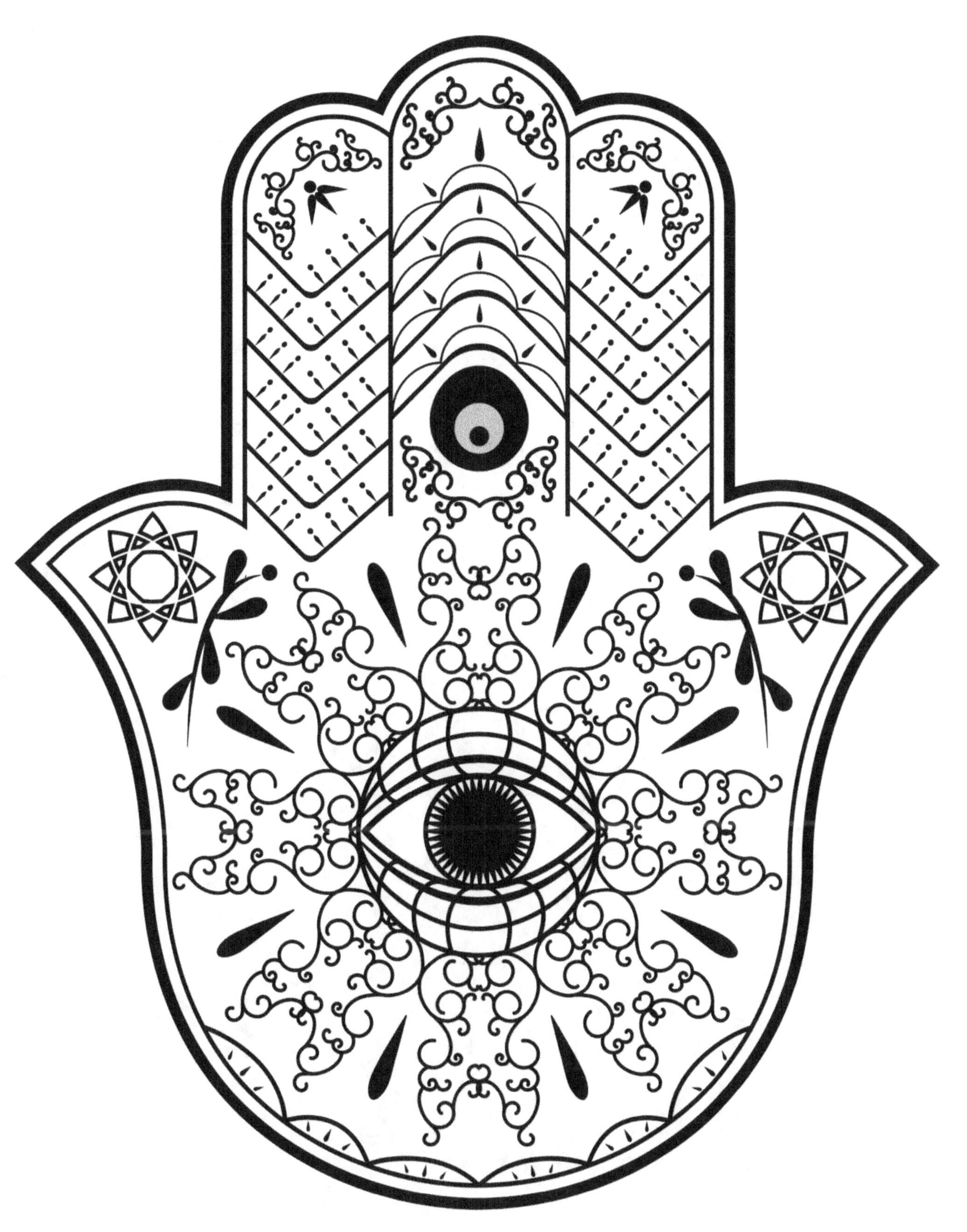

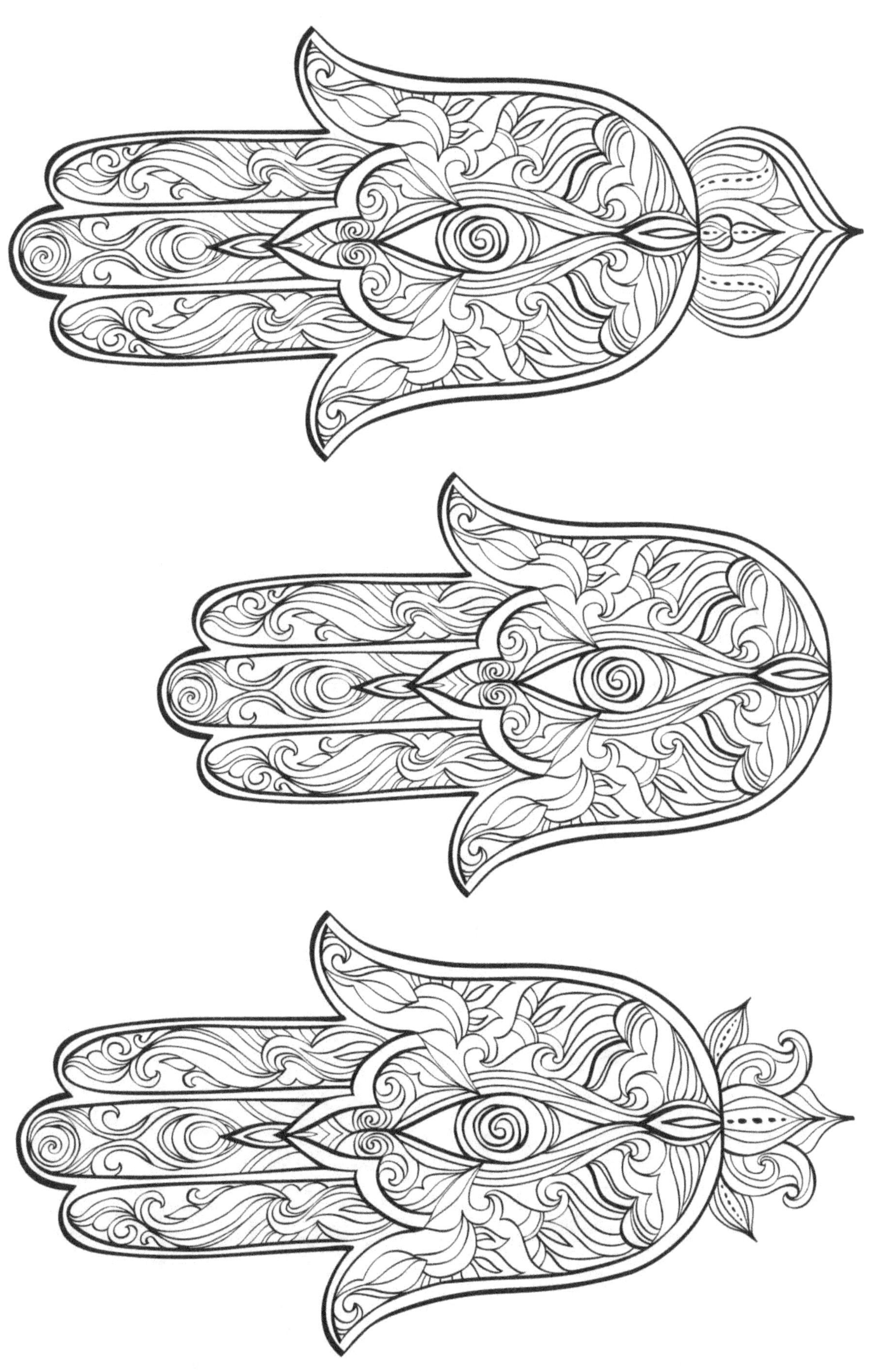

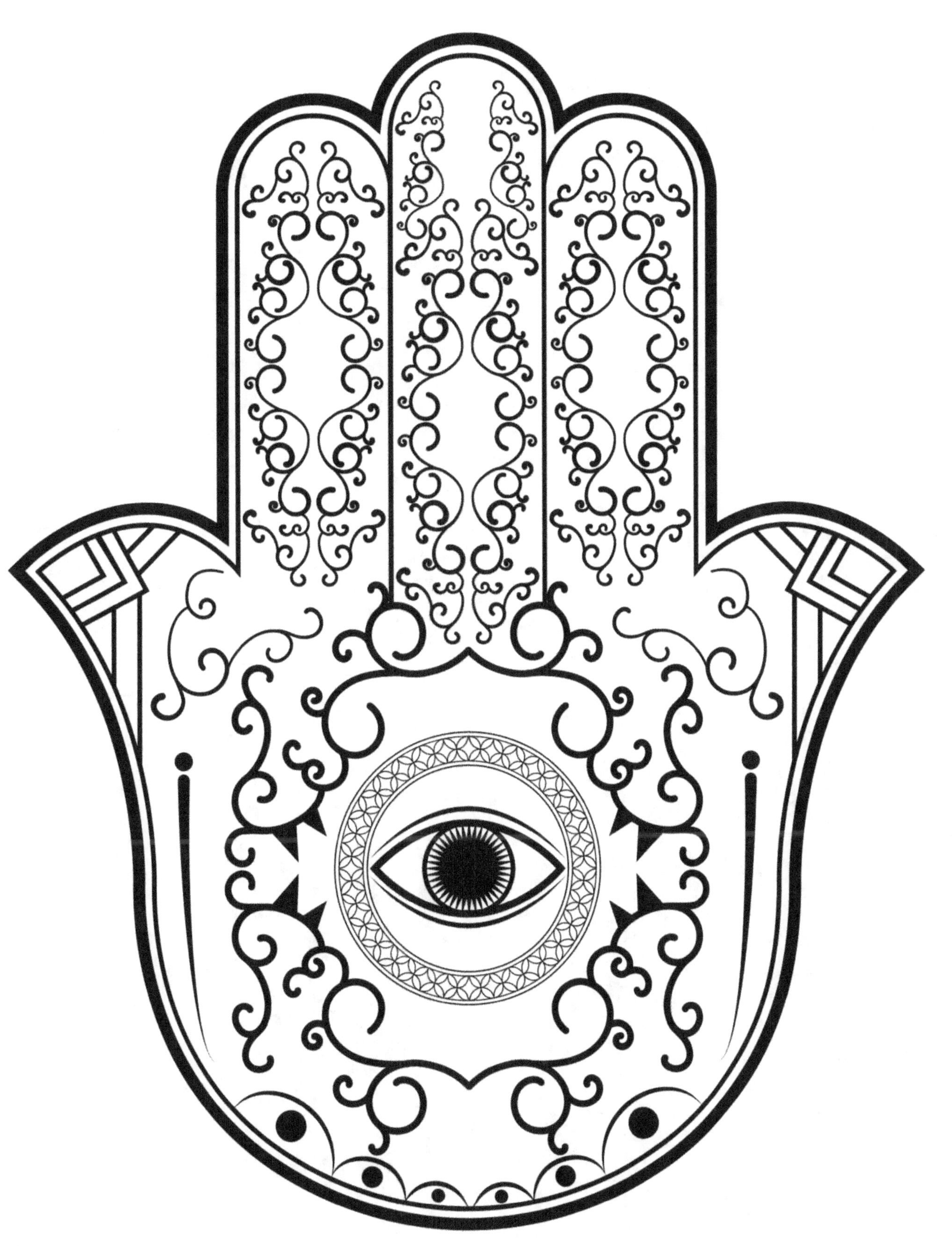

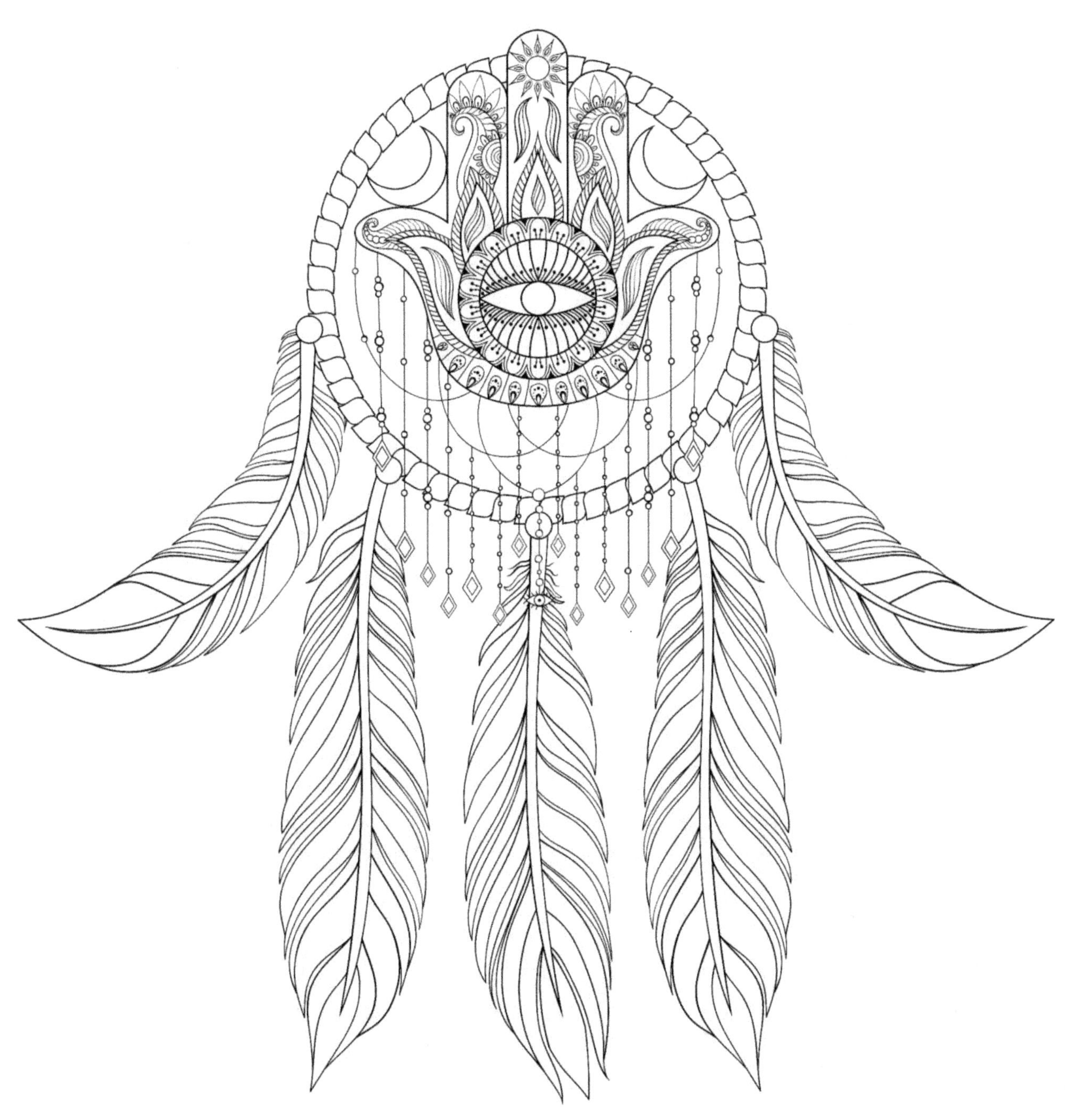

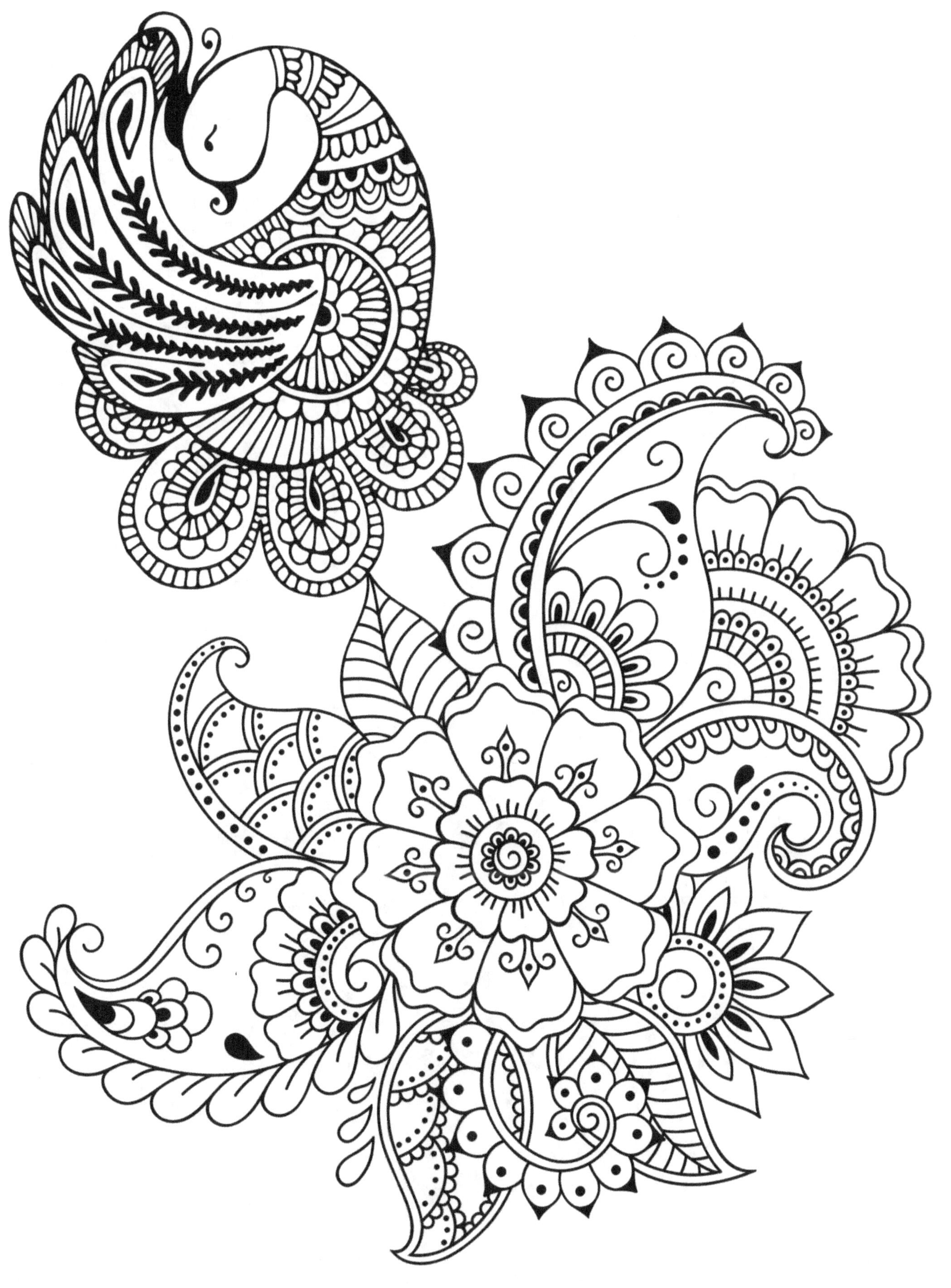

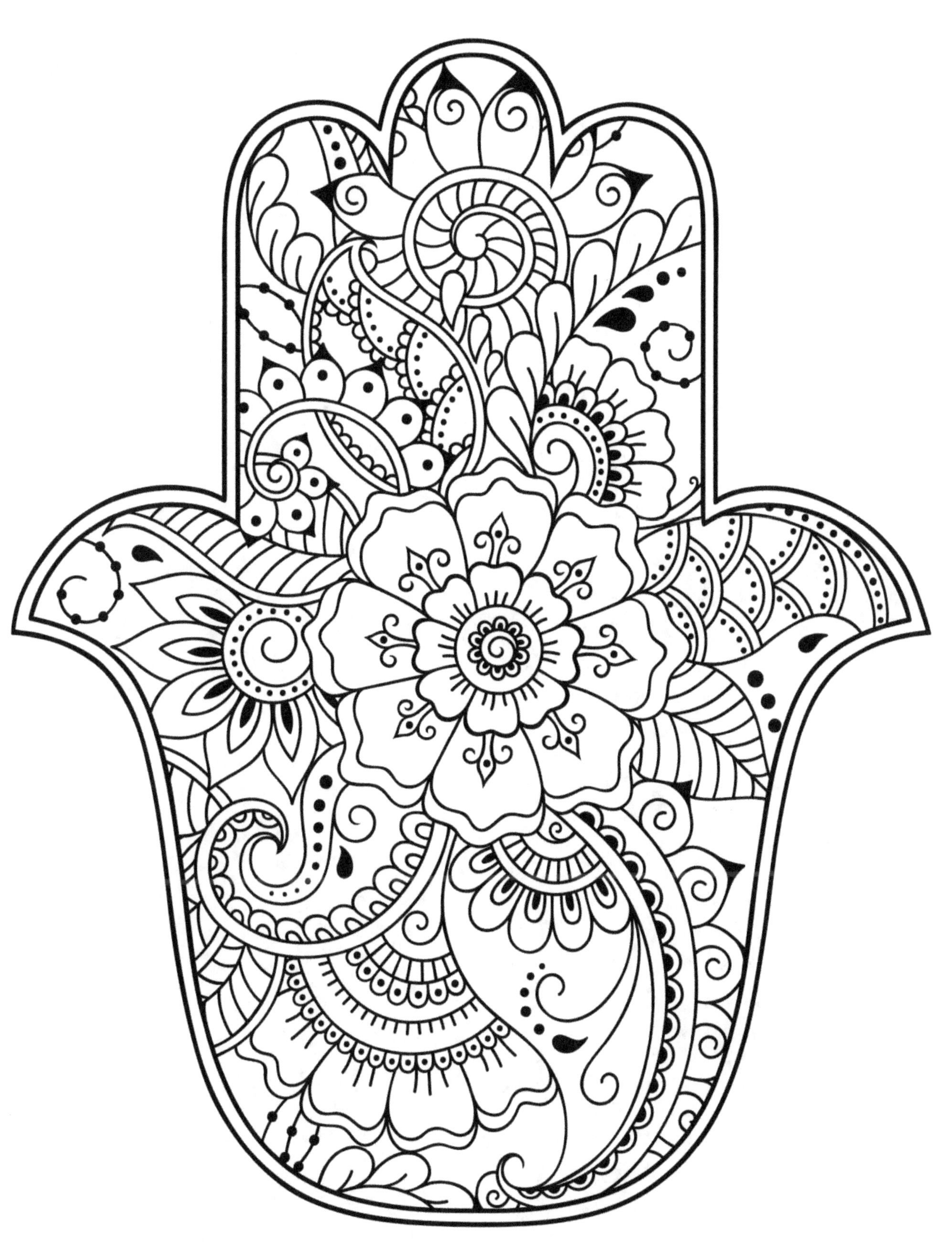

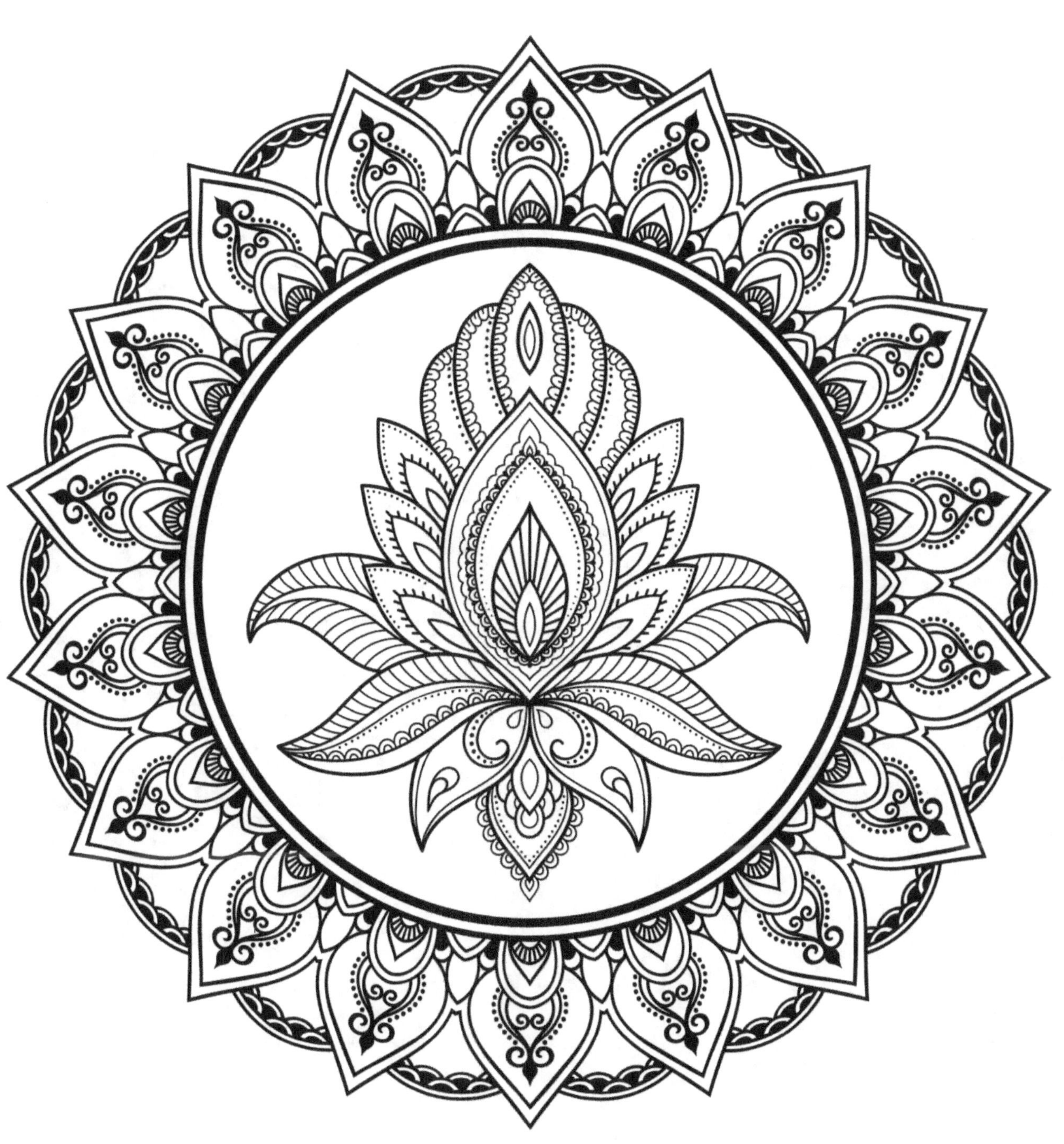

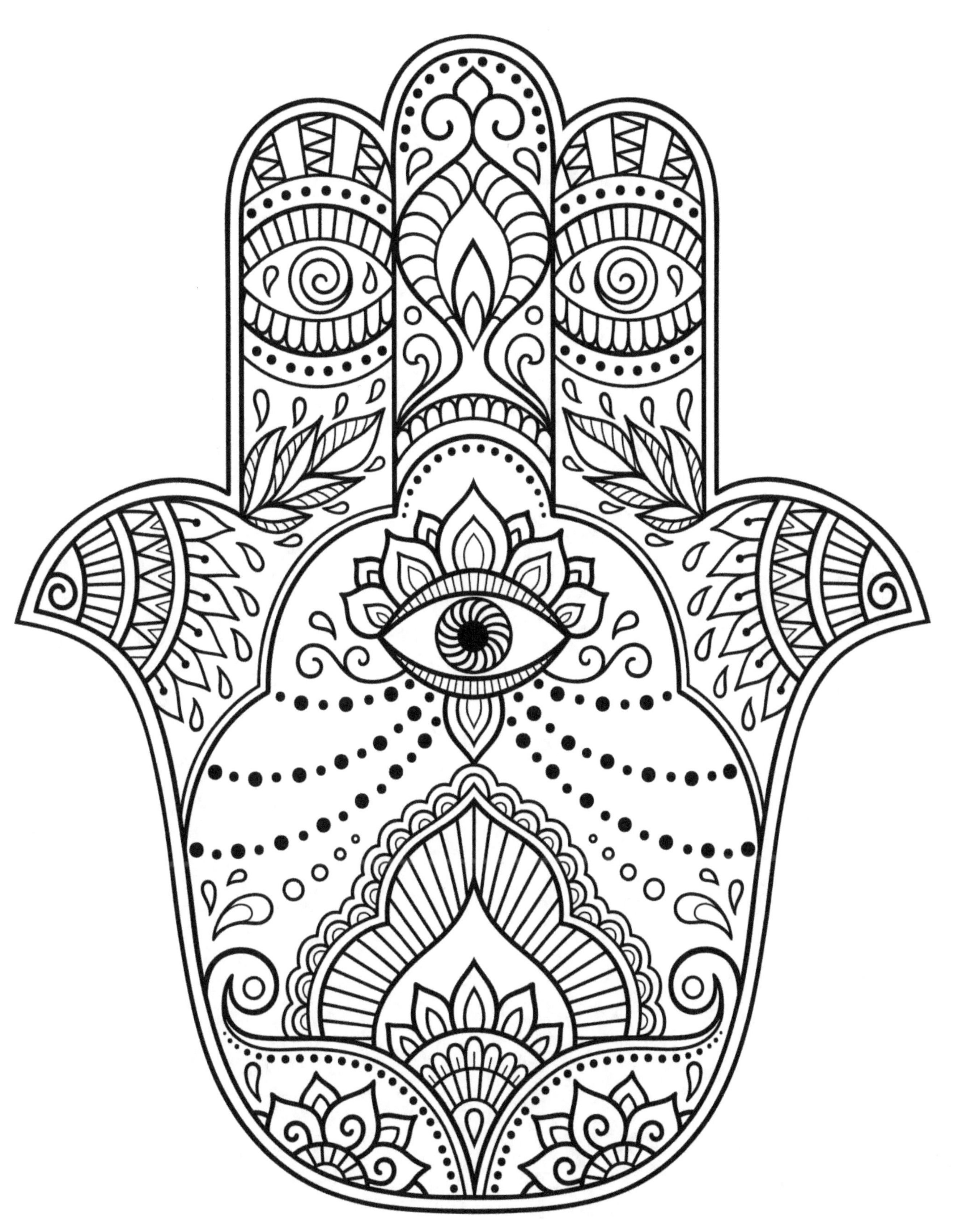

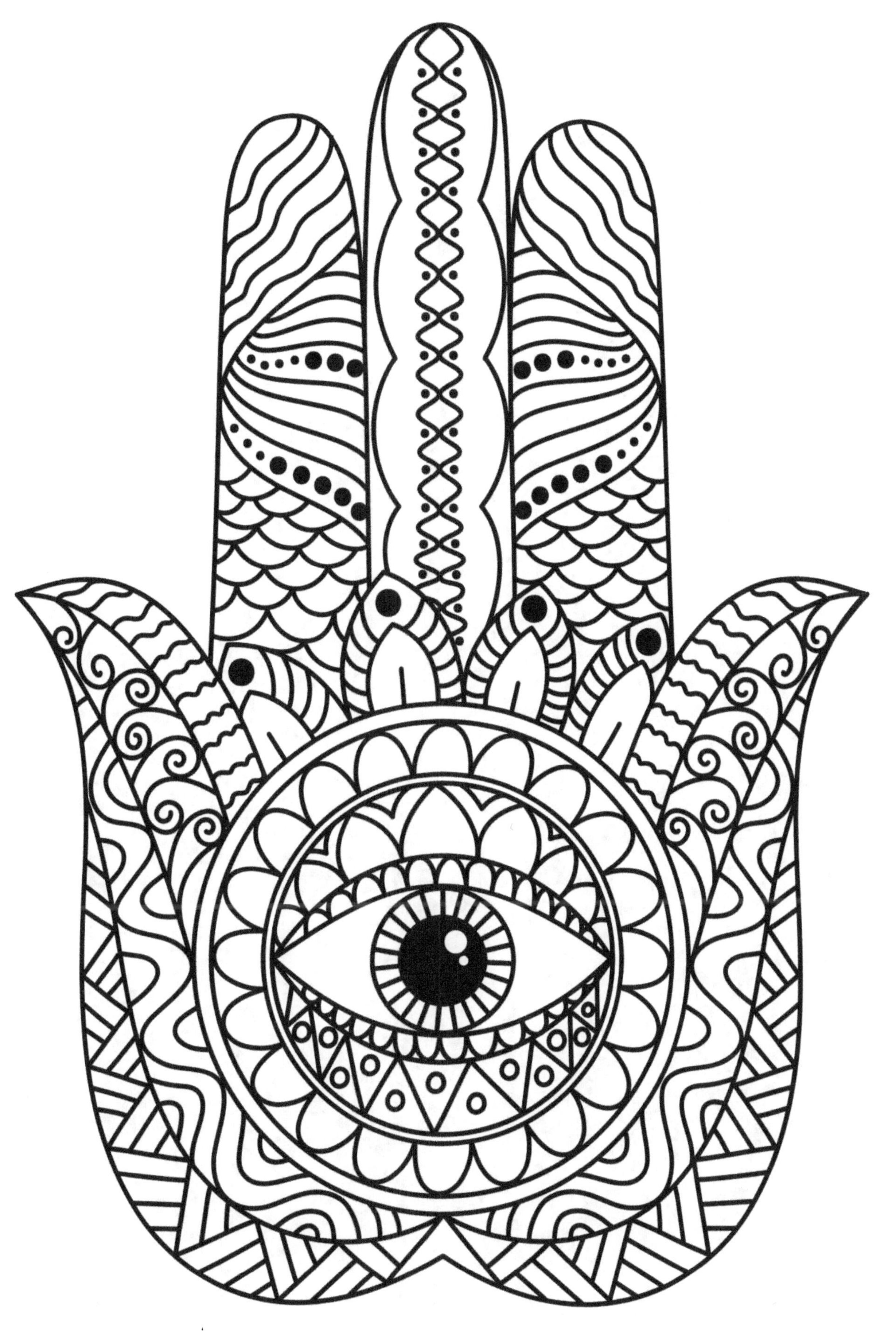

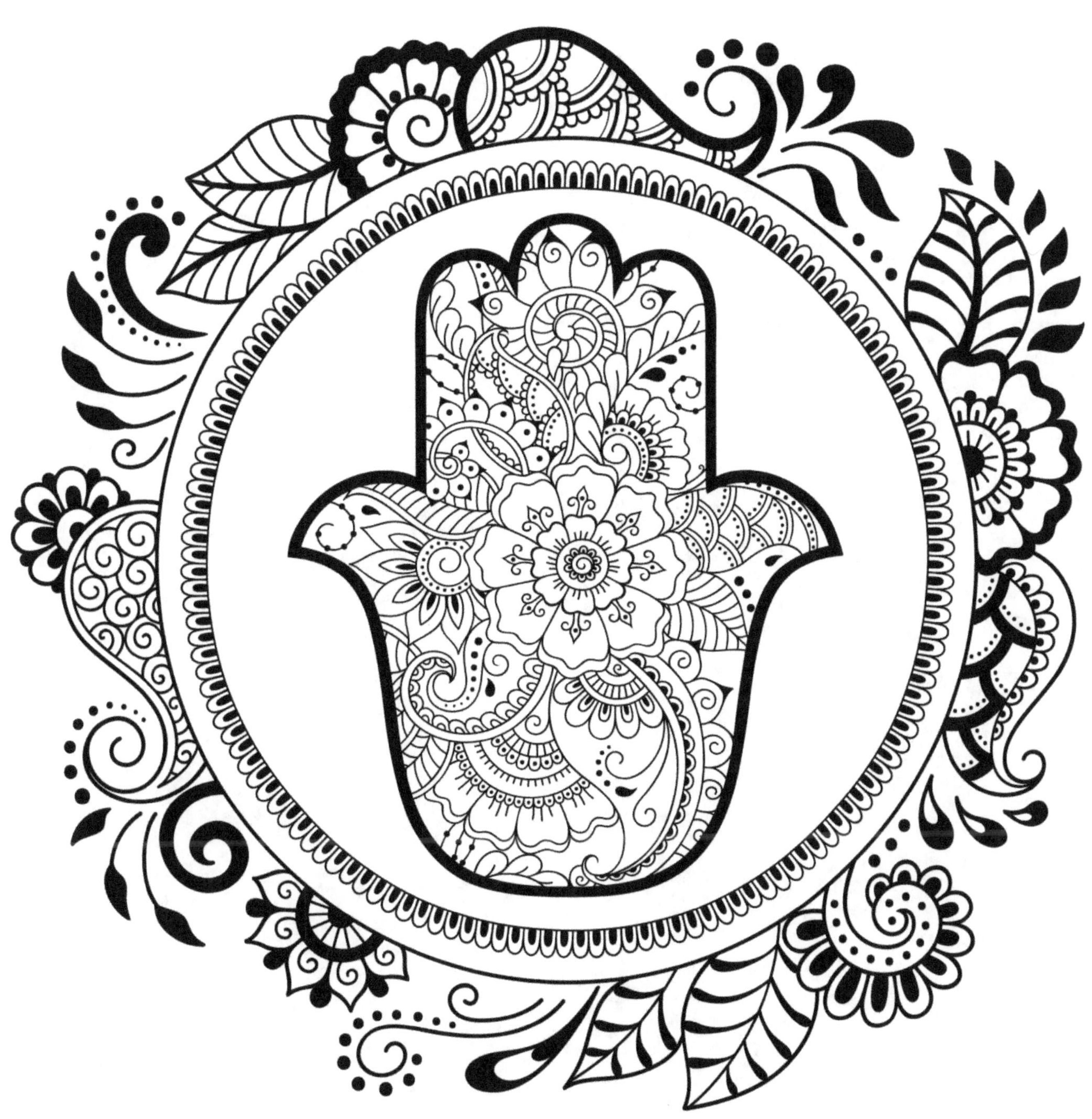

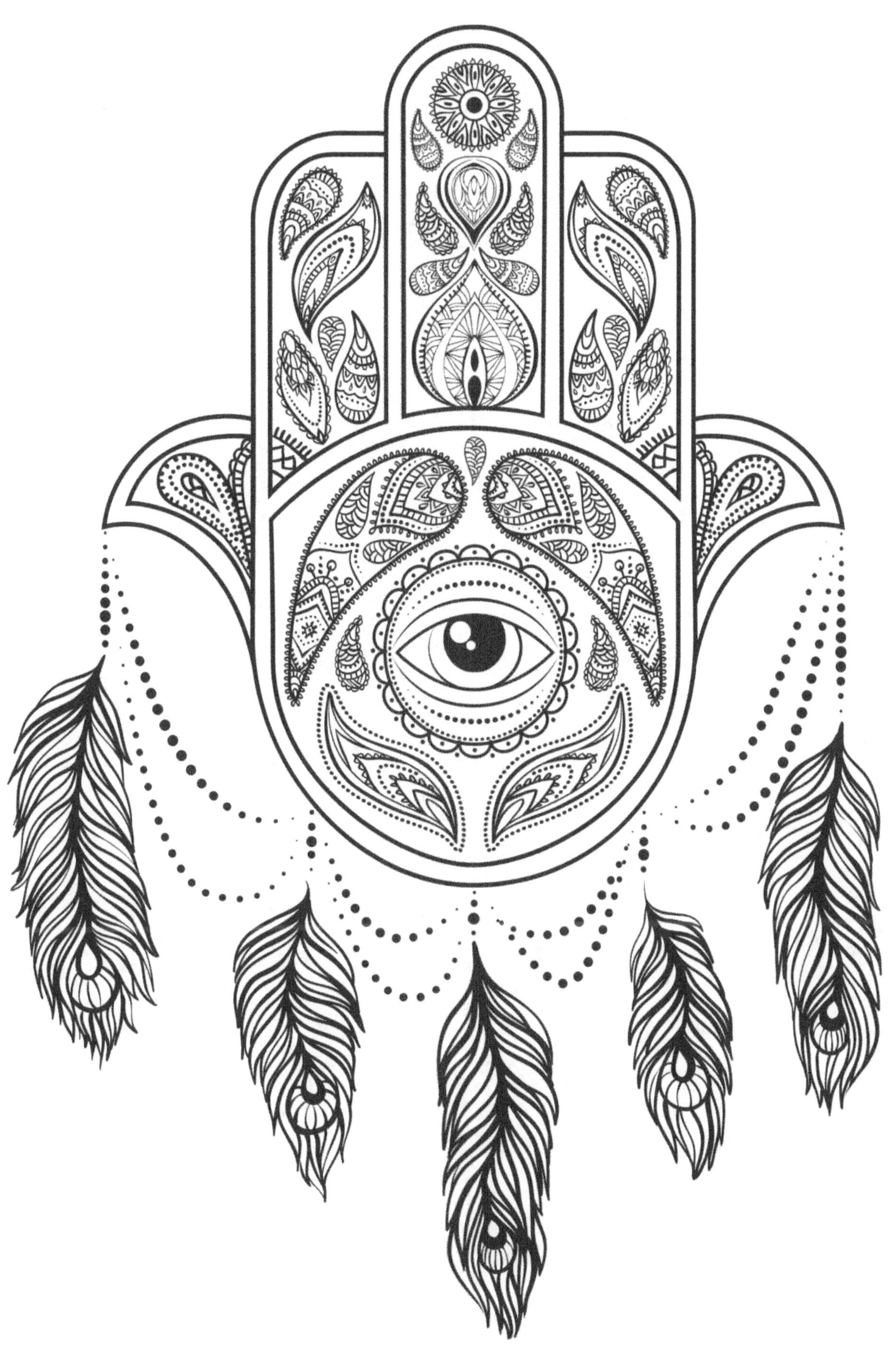

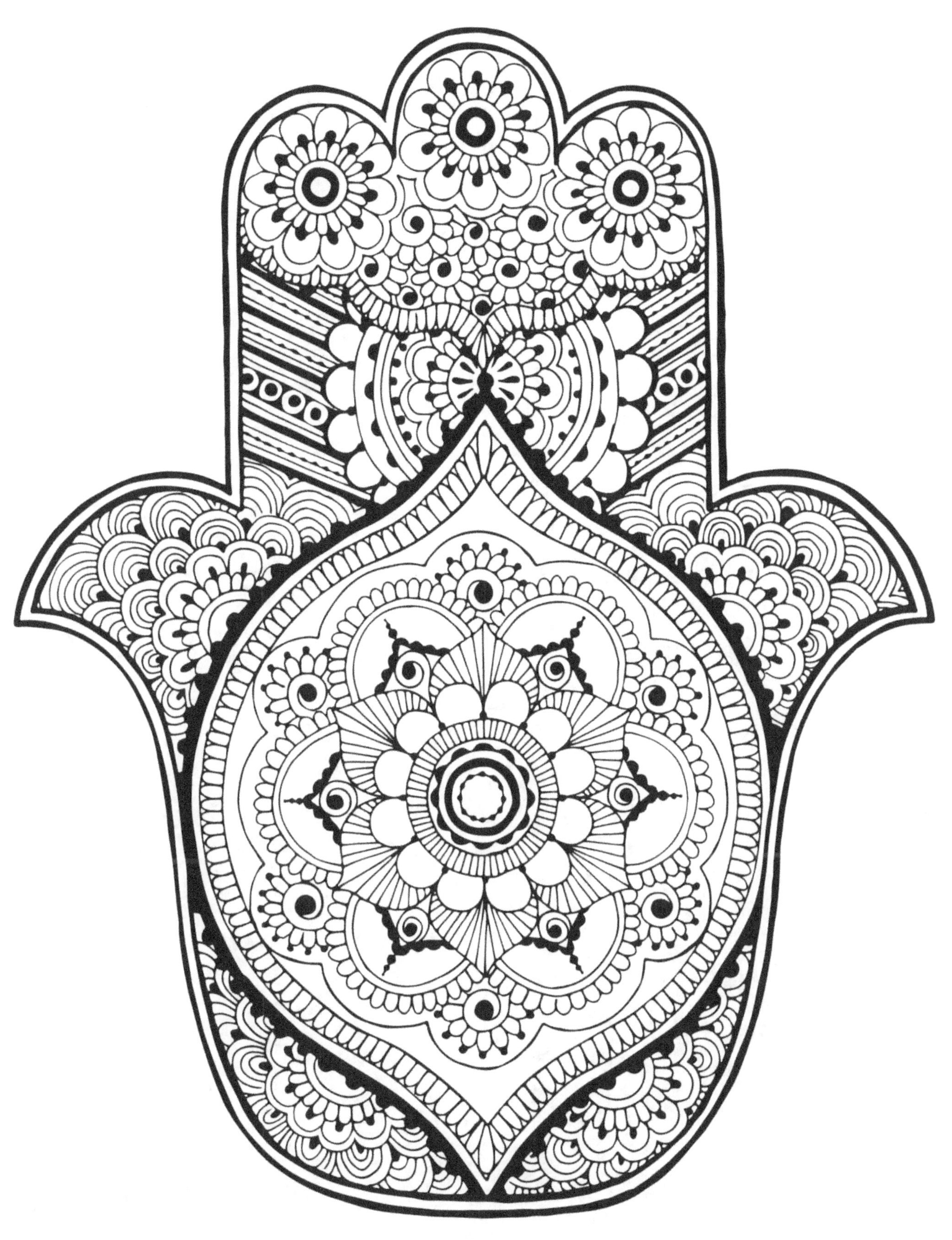

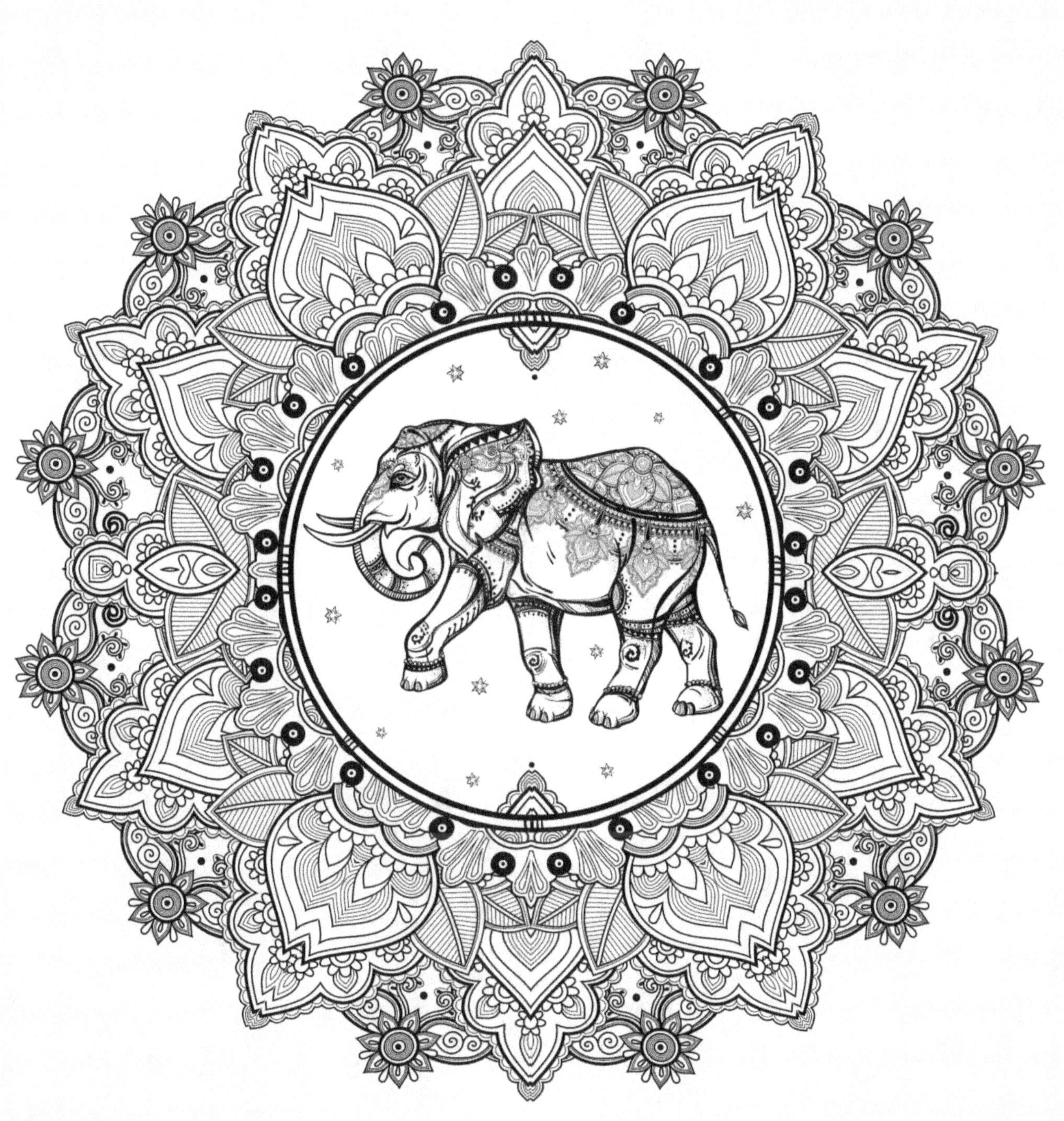

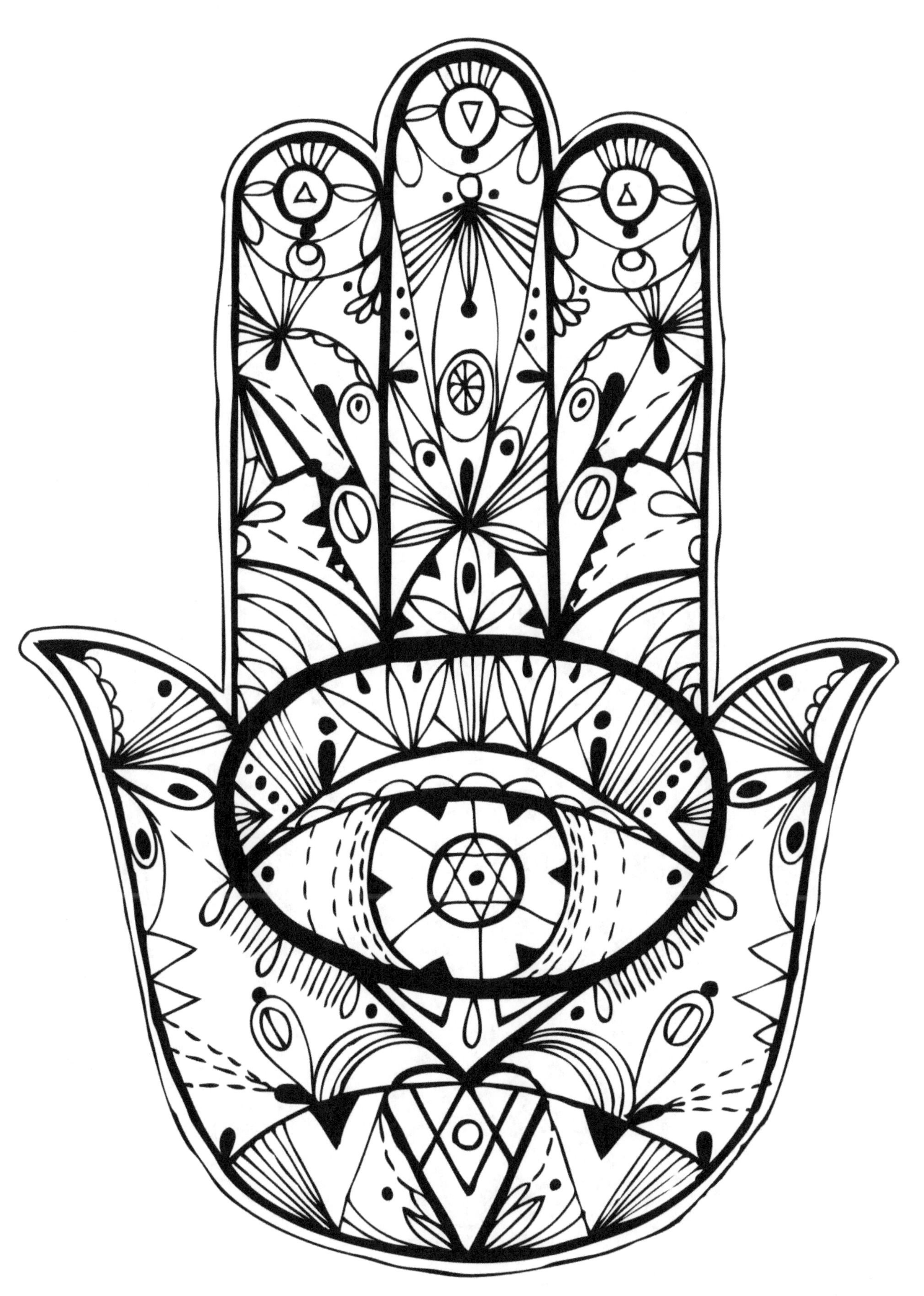